The Power Of "Retained" Profit:

How to increase stock and profit simultaneously

Martin Cole

All rights reserved. No part of this publication may be reproduced, distributed, or transmitted in any form or by any means, including photocopying, recording, or other electronic or mechanical methods, without the prior written permission of the publisher, except in the case of brief quotations embodied in critical reviews and certain other noncommercial or casual uses permitted by copyright law.

Copyright © Martin Cole, 2022.

CONTENTS

Introduction
Definition Of stock
Brief Explanation on profit

Stock and profit
Relationship between profit and stock
Factors that determine the rate of turnover

Retained profit
What is Profit plow-back?
Benefits of Retaining profit.
Why retain earnings?
What Retained Profits are used for

Stock Revaluation
Definition of Stock Revaluation
Why is it necessary to revalue inventories
Methods of Stock Revaluation: FIFO, LIFO and WAC
Ways to inform customers about price increase

Withdrawal of profit
The Profit Retaining Strategy And Its Effect On Stock And Profit
SALES PROMOTION: A determinant of the returns on retained

_____ Profit.

Record keeping

- Record keeping
- Essential Records To Be Kept.
- Steps for keeping records
- The value of keeping accurate records
- How Credit Limits Work

The complexity of accounts as the business gets bigger

- Common problems resulting from rapid growth
- Improvement On Accounting and Management
- Skills required to sustain a business's expansion;

DEFINITION OF STOCK

A store of items ready for sale, a supply of anything ready for use, or the cash raised by a corporation through the issue of shares (Unit of stock- financial and this is not our area of concentration- are all ways to characterize stock, also known as inventory.

Additionally, each of these categories will apply to you based on the type of business you are engaged in, such as a small-scale enterprise, a factory, a retail or wholesale firm, etc.

Stock can also be defined as the raw material from which things are manufactured.
In addition to goodwill and other intangible assets, stock represents the owners' equity and the enterprise's worth.

Like the proverb "You can't give what you don't have," the sales we make in our business are restricted to the products we have in stock.

I hope you now understand what it implies, but if not, move on to the next session to clear up your uncertainty.

Brief Explanation On Profit

The returns on sales after the value (cost price) of the stock has been subtracted are referred to as PROFIT, which most people understand as Gain.

The income accumulated is what the business owner can withdraw and spend for his own needs or outside investments without it having an impact on the company (causing stock reduction).

It can be summed up as the selling price less the cost price, or the sum of the remaining funds after deducting the cost price from the selling price.

Every business in the world operates with the primary goal of profiting, not the opposite—cost price > selling price, except for charitable organizations.

The majority of business owners are unaware, however, that a significant portion of the earnings can be used to expand the company's inventory and capacity while also generating additional revenue.

The majority of business owners are unaware, however, that a significant portion of the earnings can be used to expand the company's inventory and capacity while also generating additional revenue.

RELATIONSHIP BETWEEN STOCK AND PROFIT

What is the link between stock and profit now that we are aware of what stock and profit are?
How is profit affected by the stock rate? It's really easy.

Stock is a store of items that are offered for sale, and profit is the owner's reward when the items are sold.

While it may seem simple, making a profit is more difficult than it appears. We can all desire excellent things, but there are costs involved. Several factors affect the profit and turnover rate (the number of times sales of the stock have been made);

Appropriate Management

The items in the store that will be offered for sale to customers need to be accurately and regularly monitored. Before storage, quality, amount, packing, and longevity must be examined and confirmed.

As an illustration, Mr. Reghaams Daniel purchased a box of beverages on August 5, 2020, not realizing that they would expire on November 20, 2020. Customers will return a large number of the items, particularly if Mr. Reghaams is a wholesaler.

Because the loss would be borne by the company or Mr. Reghaams Daniel and not the clients, we must make sure the items we place in storage are in good shape and worth purchasing.

Promotion of Sales

Sales promotion is a type of marketing approach where the product is advertised utilizing quick, alluring attempts to boost demand and boost sales.

Importance Of Sales Promotion

- It promotes new products, sell out current inventory, draw in additional customers, and temporarily boost sales.
- It entices potential customers to purchase the goods, sales promotion is a practical strategy for achieving short-term sales objectives.
- It Informs new clients or a new market about the brand.
- It increase sales volume steadily and meet short-term sales targets.
- It makes the product seem amazing to increase demand temporarily.

FACTORS THAT DETERMINE THE RATE OF TURNOVER

1. **Availability**: the availability of the business will also impact the pace of turnover. Make sure your consumers are aware of the times you will be available and do all in your power to never let them down. Disappointment enrages us as people, which could cause them to acquire a dislike of your company and patronize your rivals.

2. **Goodwill (good name):** the good name that has been earned by your firm will impact the degree of sales you make. A high rate of turnover is assured if a business fulfills at least two of the aforementioned criteria.

3. **Advertisement**: Through paid channels, advertising is a marketing strategy that enables you to communicate with potential clients about your goods or services.

    The purpose of advertising for a small business may be to increase brand recognition, enhance your reputation, increase interaction, produce leads, or turn prospective leads into customers.

PS: These points are merely suggestions; they do not constitute the bulk of this book's content.

RETAINED PROFIT

WHAT IS PROFIT PLOW-BACK?

If you're in business, chances are good that one of your primary motivations is to make money.

Able managers will use a percentage of annual profits to keep their businesses competitive. This capital is sometimes referred to as reinvested income or, more commonly, retained earnings.

Reinvesting your retained profits into the business is the optimum form of finance. If your enterprise is making profits, it can reinvest them to further improve profitability, productivity, or efficiency and will improve balance sheet strength.

Reinvestment is when income distributions received from an investment are plowed back into that investment instead of receiving cash. Reinvestment is a great way to significantly increase the value of a stock.

BENEFITS OF RETAINING PROFITS

1. *Increased Profit:*
Reinvesting your business is critical to any company that wants to grow and take in additional resources and capital that would otherwise go to competitors. Companies that are relatively new and still in stages of early growth are more likely to reinvest versus distribute income to shareholders or owners.

A primary business reason to reinvest in growth is to increase revenue and profit. By attracting new customers, adding new business locations, or adding new products, your business can increase its number of revenue streams and hopefully generate increased profit from them.

Adding new sources of income also helps insulate your business from the risks of operating with one primary source of income if the source dries up at some point.

2. *New Capital:*
New or developing markets, or emerging customer segments, are ripe for the taking. While small businesses especially might consider sticking to what they know and staying comfortable, the race for new capital and income streams is critical.

If your competitors gain access to those new market opportunities because they invest in growth, they also get new funds to use for marketing, which increases demand, and further reinvestment in growth going forward.

   Warren Buffett's investment career started early and in a somewhat unexpected manner.

  One of his early investments was in high school when he and a friend bought a used pinball machine for $25 and installed it in a barbershop. The game proved to be popular with the barbershop's clientele, so the entrepreneurial duo reinvested their profits to buy more pinball machines. In time, they had eight machines in several shops.

   Eventually, they sold their venture, and Buffett used his portion of the proceeds to buy stock and then launch another business. By the time he was 26, he'd accrued $174,000 -- or 1.4 million dollars worth of value in today's market.

   Warren Buffett materialized the two benefits of profit reinvestment as stated above in the book.

Retained Earnings are the accumulated portion of a company's profits that are set aside for reinvestment rather than being taken out for the owner's personal use.

These funds are typically allocated for debt repayment or utilized for working capital (daily petty expenses), fixed asset acquisitions (e.g., a motor van for delivery of goods), furniture and fittings, land, etc.

Example of Retained Earnings:
On items valued at $25,000, Mr. Festus Brown made a profit of $6,000. A week later, he spent $400 on a typewriter, 2000 dollars on a motor van, and 40 dollars on stationary and fuel.

The retained profit in this instance is $2,440. The firm will positively benefit from this!

WHAT RETAINED PROFITS ARE USED FOR

Retaining these profits can be used for a variety of things, such as investing in new machinery and equipment, doing research and development, or doing other things that might lead to future business expansion.

The goal of this investment back into the business is to generate even higher profits in the future.

A corporation may frequently pay retained earnings to shareholders as dividends or engage in share buybacks if it does not think it can generate a satisfactory return on investment from those funds (i.e., earn more than its cost of capital).

If gains are reinvested in a company, they are put to use expanding or improving that company.

Advantages of Retained Profit.

Since there are no fees or interest payments, unlike loans, it is an inexpensive form of funding.

- Utilizing retained revenues is quick and adaptable.
- There are no restrictions on how you can use the funds, and you won't have to wait for a lender to approve your application. Retained earnings can be invested in different area of the company, new equipment, or an increased workforce.
- Your future earnings may grow if you retain earnings. Unlike a loan, the money you spend will not be deducted from your future profits as interest.

- You are investing to increase your company's profitability.

The benefits of using retained earnings as a source of funding include the following:

(I) An organization's permanent source of funding is retained earnings.

(ii) There are no explicit costs associated with it in the shape of interest, dividends, or flotation costs.

(iii) There is more operational freedom and flexibility because the funds are generated internally.

(iv) It increases the company's ability to take on unforeseen losses.

(v) It might cause the market price of a company's equity shares to rise.

Page intentionally left blank

STOCK RE- VALUATION.

It's crucial to maintain a careful eye on your inventory value if you run a business with large inventory needs. The net total value of all the items that are currently in your inventory makes up your inventory value.

Therefore, maintaining a successful product-based business requires regular and prompt inventory tracking and revaluation.

Inventory revaluation is the process of adjusting inventory costs to account for changes in recorded costs. Exchange currency fluctuations, supply chain disruptions, obsolescence, damage or spoilage, among other factors, may be to blame for these changes.

Businesses value their stock for a number of reasons, including financial reporting, tax planning, and business judgment.

Revaluing inventory improves accuracy and aids in tax and financial planning for a business.

Additionally, it is crucial in helping to make important business decisions.

WHY IS IT NECESSARY TO REVALUE INVENTORY?

Here are some of the factors that make inventory revaluation important for managing a firm that sells products and why you should start doing it right away:

- An interruption in the supply chain:

Your supply chain is more susceptible to failures if any of the products in your inventory, which are made from a variety of raw materials, are unavailable. It is therefore wise to have several sources for each element.

- Variable Demand

There is no room for complacency when it comes to forecasting future demands in the increasingly globalized and competitive society we currently live in. Due to excessive inventory levels and a sharp decline in demand, some businesses have had to file for bankruptcy.

It is advisable to regularly perform inventory revaluation in order to prevent this. It enables businesses to maintain a low inventory and respond to sudden market changes quicker than their rivals.

The importance of inventory valuation.

Inventory valuation involves many steps in addition to identifying the unsold items. To get a final value, you also need a rate that you may multiply by the amount.

You might have paid various rates for these things during the course of the year, therefore you need to decide on a method to determine a standard cost.

A revaluation is an increase in the value of assets, products, or particularly the currency relative to a predetermined baseline. Devaluation, which refers to a downward adjustment, is its opponent.

METHODS OF STOCK REVALUATION

Inventory valuation can be done using FIFO (First In, First Out), LIFO (Last In, First Out), or WAC (Weighted Average Cost).

You presume that the first products purchased will be the first to depart the warehouse when using FIFO. In other words, under FIFO, the items will be deducted from the first list of goods that entered your warehouse or store whenever you make a sale.

In LIFO, you assume the exact opposite: that the objects that arrived last are the ones that left first.

The WAC approach makes use of the item's annual average cost. By dividing the total cost by the total number of units bought during the year, the average cost per unit is determined. A revaluation in an increase in the value of assets, products, or particularly the currency relative to a predetermined baseline. Devaluation, which refers to a downward adjustment, is its opponent.

WAYS TO INFORM CUSTOMERS ABOUT A PRICE INCREASE.

It's unfair for a consumer to learn all of a sudden that the price of their product has increased. Send a price increase letter to all of your list customers who use that product or service to inform them of the change if there is a price increase. To personalize the process, if at all possible, address the letters to each customer.

Several tips are as follows;

1. **Speak with them directly**.
Imagine if, without your knowledge or permission, the monthly cost of your Spotify Premium

subscription went from $9.99 to $14.99. I assume you would be quite furious. It's unfair for a consumer to learn all of a sudden that the price of their product has increased.

2. **Send a price increase letter** to all of your list customers who use that product or service to inform them of the change if there is a price increase. To personalize the process, if at all possible, address the letters to each customer.

3. **Inform clients properly in advance.**
It's important to give your clients plenty of time to adjust to the price increase. Once you've informed them of the situation, you should keep them informed because they might need to reevaluate their budget or consider other possibilities. Encourage them to order one or more products as well before the price hike takes effect.

4. **Remind them that more expensive items are of higher quality.**

Customers may be perplexed by the need for a price increase, particularly if they have been buying the same item for months or years. It is crucial that you emphasize how important product quality is.

Products typically cost more because of higher operating expenses, higher employee salaries, or higher costs for raw materials. Sometimes you have to increase the price in order to maintain the same degree of great quality.Describe the justification for the price rise.

Explaining the reason for the price rise will make it clear that you're rising them to preserve the product's quality.

For instance, businesses that use certain raw materials are compelled to raise the pricing for the items they produce when these materials grow more expensive and scarce. Customers will see that you are willing to be open and honest if you explain it to them.

5. Before informing clients of the price rise, make sure the entire company is aware of it. It would be embarrassing for a front-line employee to mistakenly charge a client the incorrect amount as a result of their employer's failure to inform them of a change.

Even if all staff members were informed of the problem, they should all be in agreement with the pricing disparity, the justification, and the logistics going ahead. In this manner, your firm will speak with a unified voice.

6. Encourage clients to contact you with any additional queries or issues.
Make certain your clients receive all the information they need. Lack of knowledge could lead them to defect to a rival offering lower costs. Assure them that if they have any more queries or worries about the price rise, they may always get in

touch with anyone at your organization, even senior executives.

WITHDRAWAL OF PROFIT

When a sole proprietor takes money out of the firm or business for personal reasons or use, this is a withdrawal of profit. The effect of this action is :

    Increase of owner's personal account

    The neutrality of the Stock account, since it's a net profit(Expenses subtracted from Profit, such as tax and fuel expenses)

However, like it's stated in chapter two, if profit is retained to business, the stock will not remain neutral, it increases. As a result of this, the profit that will be made on the next sales will increase by some rate which will be to the benefit of the business and owner.

This is just a no-brainer strategy but not so many business owners know about it.

THE PROFIT RETAINING STRATEGY AND ITS EFFECT ON STOCK AND PROFIT.

I often implore many of my friends and co-workers in a diverse line of trade to make sure Profit making isn't their only aim.

Profit-making shouldn't avoid you from increasing your stock. Expanding your business *capacity and stock* should be **one** of the primary aims and objectives of a business owner.

Why? This is because the more you retain profits, the larger your stock gets; as your stock increases (with good management skills and accurate record keeping), the higher the rate of turnover (how many times sales are made) because the business' capacity has been increased, and the higher the rate of turnover, the higher the amount of profit.

This is just a short-but-valuable strategy a business can adopt to enhance a turnaround in the scale of business. This can turn a small-scale business into a multi-million-making business. This doesn't have to do with investment in external businesses or platforms

Take for instance Mr. Brian, owner of a soft drink wholesale depot. He sells an estimated number of 60,000 packs of coca-cola in a month - the rate of turnover and makes a profit of 5000 USD. The stock costs 78,000 USD. Retaining his profit brings about a new capital of 83,000 USD, which enables him to buy 63,850 packs of coca-cola into his stock, approximately.

Obviously, there has been a very significant increase in his stock and this earns him a profit of 5,600 USD estimated.

He has benefited from this strategy in two ways; his profits have increased likewise his stock. Now if Mr. Brian, does this five times before drawing out the profit for his personal use with excellent sales promotion strategies too, his business will be up with flying colors.

SALES PROMOTION: A determinant of the returns on retained profit.

Excellent sales promotion strategies must be adopted to get the fruitful pry of profit reinvestment.

Advertisements must be improved to bring in more customers, the business must be available during expected working hours depending on the nature of your business, goodwill must be earned, and discounts on bulk purchases from customers should be introduced.

Record keeping

Recordkeeping is an important—and occasionally challenging—aspect of running a successful small business for entrepreneurs worldwide.

It's not simply smart business to keep accurate records of your earnings, spending, payroll, and financial transactions. You can have peace of mind from it, track your progress toward goals, and save time and money.

Recording Basic recordings consist of:
Enterprise costs
Records of sales
Receivables account
Payables accounts
Customer list, Vendor list, Employee list
Tax papers
Invoices
Ordering documents
Receipts
Statements of banks

Contracts

By maintaining these records, you'll be able to:
1. Be aware of the investment needed to manufacture your product or service.
2. Fix prices
3. Comparison of anticipated and actual costs track spending
4. Choose wisely when making purchases.
5. Prepare for tax season.
6. Information on clients and staff is readily available.
7. Determine the anticipated profit.

Essential Records To Be Kept.

Establish a system for monitoring transactions and other information to begin the record-keeping process. It might be done electronically, on paper, or a combination of the two. Some of the most crucial documents to have are listed below:

1. **Sales log:** This log should detail how much you sell every day, every week, and every month, as well as the date, the nature of each sale, and how much it costs.

2. **Accounts payable** log: An accounts payable log lists the money that a corporation owes other people or companies. Include the amount due, who is owed it to, when payment is due, and the date you made the payment.
 You won't be charged for the same good or service more than once if you maintain an effective accounts payable log.
 Additionally, keeping track of the savings provided for early payments might help you remember to take advantage of them.

3. **Accounts receivable Log**: An accounts receivable log keeps track of the money clients or customers owe a company for items or services they received. This record comprises a list of the clients

who owe you money, their outstanding balance, and the due date for payment. Additionally, you can include a list of clients that shouldn't be given credit based on previous payment defaults. Include the date, the customer's name, the amount, the date it was collected, and the status of each entry.

4. **Log of business expenses:** In this log, you'll list all of your company's expenses, including rent, electricity, staff pay, and supplies. The record ought to have the date, details on each expense, and the total cost.

5. **A purchase order**: a written statement that a buyer has placed an order and has agreed to pay the seller for the future sale of a particular good or service.

6. **Contracts**: Whether you enter into a supply contract with a business partner, rent a new piece of equipment, or purchase business insurance, you should save a copy of the contract for your records.

You can also avoid future disputes by keeping a copy of any contracts.

7.   **List Of Customers:** Keeps track of your consumers' information so you can promote sales or new products, depending on your industry. List the client's name, purchased items, contact information (email, phone), and, as well as a postal or shipping address. To safeguard this private data, you should have a security strategy in place.

Some records may need to be kept on file even after they are no longer necessary for regular business activities to remain compliant and prevent legal issues.

For instance, you might wish to maintain copies of all of your contracts for up to seven years, but you should likely keep auditor reports, annual statements, and retirement plan documents forever.

STEPS FOR KEEPING RECORDS

1. Pick a bookkeeping technique.
2. Create your general ledger.
3. Create a business account.
4. Keep track of all transactions involving money.
5. The books should be in order.
6. Create financial reports
7. Make a schedule for your bookkeeping.
8. Keep documents in a safe place. .

THE VALUE OF KEEPING ACCURATE RECORDS

Keeping accurate records is essential for a successful business. Every person who does business must maintain records, and the better organized the records are, the more information you can extract from them. Good record-keeping will assist with the following:

1. Track the development of your company

2. Your financial statements should be ready.

3. Find the source of the receipts.

Let's break into each of the aforementioned points to show why having solid records is essential.

1. **Track the development of your company**:

You must maintain accurate records if you want to track the progress of your company. Records can show if your company is growing or shrinking, whether one product is selling better than another, which costs you can cut or eliminate, and how you may boost your profit.

You may better your chances of running a successful business by keeping accurate records, which will assist you in finding the answers to those questions.

2. **Your financial statements should be ready**:

You need correct records to prepare financial statements. You may run your firm with the aid of financial statements.

Examples of financial reports you need to monitor your firm include the cash flow statement, balance sheet, and income statement (profit and loss). Financial statements are frequently requested from banks or creditors, so it's critical to keep correct books and file them on time.

3. **Find the source of the receipts:**

Income from operations or sales, interest income, or proceeds from the sale of company property are just a few ways that money might enter a corporation. It's critical to comprehend the source of receipts (incoming funds) to accurately report income on tax returns.

Your financial records will show where the money is coming from and how it should be disclosed on your tax filings. Examples of proof of income documentation include:

1. Slips from the bank,
2. Duplicates of client checks
3. Cassettes from cash registers
4. Invoices
5. Charge slips for credit cards.

HOW DOES CREDIT LIMIT WORK?

The maximum amount of credit available to a customer is known as a credit limit. It is employed to reduce the amount of loss a company will endure if a client refuses to pay. The credit department decides how much a credit limit is.

The credit limit's size is determined by several variables, including the following:

- A credit rating agency's calculation of a customer's credit score.

- Payment history of the client with the business.

- Financial performance and position of the customer as disclosed in its financial statements.

- Whether there are any personal guarantees or other forms of the collateral present.

- When a customer requests an abnormally big order, senior management or the sales manager may put pressure on the credit department to raise the credit limit so they can record a sizable sale.

While doing so may boost reported sales, there is a greater chance of suffering a substantial bad debt loss.

Typical Credit Limit Example

For illustration, a vendor gives a client a $5,000 credit limit. The client uses credit to make transactions totaling $3,000, lowering the credit limit to $2,000 as a result. At this point, the customer can make additional purchases of $2,000 on credit; however, to make a greater purchase on credit, a portion of the existing sum must be paid off.

THE COMPLEXITY OF OF ACCOUNTS AS BUSINESS GETS BIGGER.

You must conduct research and develop a growth strategy for your company. Your company may run into issues with finances, the law, staffing, resources, and suppliers if it expands or grows too quickly. Sustainable business growth is necessary for success.

COMMON PROBLEMS RESULTING FROM RAPID BUSINESS GROWTH

1. Shortly, you might overrun your space. There may not be enough space for everyone to work productively.

2. If employees are unable to handle the increased workload, morale may suffer. Productivity might drop.
There might not be enough money to cover the costs of expansion. Your workplace and workers will be under more strain if you take on more and more work to increase your revenue.

Under pressure, management may be acting reactively rather than proactively.

3. Your goods and services can become of lower quality, which would result in more complaints from customers. You can even lose clients to your rivals.

The high workloads could lead to an increase in staff turnover. As employees leave, important knowledge could be lost. It costs time and money to recruit and train new employees. Your company can go out of touch with what rivals are doing.

Accounting and Management Improvements

1. **Reconciliation**: is the process of comparing transactions and activity to supporting records promptly. Reconciling also entails settling any differences that might have been found.

Reconciliation is an accounting procedure used to confirm that the money actually spent and the amount reported as leaving an account after a fiscal period is the same. Reconciliation is a routine task done by people and corporations to look for mistakes or fraud.

As part of best practices for cash flow management, regular bank and credit reconciliations should be carried out. When reconciliations are not carried out frequently or predictably, it offers room for fraud in addition to cash mismanagement.

Ensure that lower-level accounting and bookkeeping professionals complete reconciliations promptly. They should typically be carried out at least once every month (although there may be circumstances under which an organization could choose to do them less frequently).

Businesses with high traffic and those who are more vulnerable to fraud might even think about performing daily reconciliations.

Keep in mind that routine reconciliations will help the organization get ready for the year-end close as well.

2. **Improving the Budgeting Process**: A budget is a structured projection of revenue and expenses based on goals and plans for the future.
To put it another way, a budget is a document that management creates to project revenues and costs for a future period based on their objectives for the company.

In addition to developing financial discipline, creating a budget offers a wealth of advantages for the business, making it a cornerstone for efficient financial leadership. However, budgeting is an area where many businesses fall short. Either they overpay compared to the budget or they construct one with inaccurate or missing information.

Understanding income, fixed expenditures, variable spending, and anticipated costs are necessary for creating a budget. The budget may be off if one of these elements is absent, reported incorrectly, or anticipated incorrectly.

The budget should be reviewed when it has been finished, adjusted in light of the comments received, and then approved by leadership. Make sure each team is acknowledged and included equitably, and gain support from important employees.

Instead of just rolling over the budget from the previous year, examine your budgeting process to find areas where it may be made better. Include a review of past notable budget outliers in the next budgeting process if there have been any.

3. **Creating formal policies for accounts receivable:** Create procedures in writing for submitting invoices and pursuing collections. Establish explicit guidelines that adhere to the revenue recognition principle for when invoices are sent. Create a collection strategy and decide how you will handle late payments as well. It is better to have a plan in place for how you will handle unpaid accounts receivable (AR) in advance.

Skills required to sustain a business's expansion include:

Specialized experience
Broad commercial knowledge
Current technological know-how
Communication abilities
Flexibility and adaptability.
Possessing leadership qualities.
Focus on providing good customer service.

www.ingramcontent.com/pod-product-compliance
Lightning Source LLC
Chambersburg PA
CBHW050315220526
45465CB00005B/1995